MEDICAL MARIJUANA:
THE SIMPLE TRUTH

Stephen T. Radentz

Disclaimer

Here is some legal information I must put in the book, according to my attorney:

I am not a doctor. I am not giving health advice. I am just giving you some basic facts about a very healthy plant. The information contained in this book is for general information and educational purposes only. It does not constitute medical advice. Therefore, any reliance you place on such information is strictly at your own risk. Please check with your medical doctor before starting or changing your medical routine.

This booklet is dedicated to the 27 million people who have an opioid disorder and the 118,000 who die from taking opioids every year (according to the World Health Organization), as well as the thousands of people who are living a life free of opioid-based medication because of cannabis.

I must also thank my parents, who never gave up on me, and thank my dad for teaching me what *whole gob lot* means (more than a lot :)).

Table of Contents

Preface

Marijuana, pot, weed, hemp, cannabis. The many names of a mysterious plant.

My first experience with marijuana was in 1976, when a couple of older friends took me out to smoke pot. We smoked six joints that night. All I remember is that I was hot (it was February in St. Louis), my eyes were extremely bloodshot, and there might have been some giggling involved. That night, I unknowingly fell in love with a medicinal plant.

Throughout high school, I partied heavily, and marijuana was always around. I was considered a "burnout" even though I played sports, and although I had friends in most cliques, most people associated me with marijuana.

I loved the feeling I got from smoking pot. It took my mind away from the stresses of life. I had what people would today call attention deficit hyperactivity disorder (ADHD), and cannabis helped calm me down.

I felt that marijuana was helping me.
However, my parents, teachers, and the police were always trying to stop me from using it. I fought with my parents over the killer weed. I was arrested for carrying marijuana. I was even asked to move out of my parents' house because of my supposed addiction to cannabis.

I never completely abandoned marijuana, and now, 40 years later, it's still a large part of my life. It has created some amazing memories, as well as some extremely difficult challenges. Had my environment helped me embrace cannabis instead of being ostracized for it, perhaps some events in my life would have turned out differently.

Over the years, I would periodically step away from using cannabis. When my kids were young, I mostly abstained or hid in the shadows. However, every time I walked away from marijuana; I was drawn back to the plant.

In 2004, having fallen and fractured my spine, I began a slow death spiral as an addict to legal opioids. For the next eight years, I battled depression and stomach ulcers. At the end of every month, I would face withdrawal symptoms, as well as the fear of running out of medication.

At one point, I was prescribed 1,080 pills a month! More than half were opioids, while the rest were prescribed to fix the problems the opioids were causing.

In 2012, I was rushed to the emergency room with bleeding ulcers. This happened again in 2014. I had lost almost 40 pounds over eighteen months. I was killing myself.

One night at the end of the month in 2014, I was facing imminent withdrawal sickness. Let me tell you: withdrawal sucks! I was not eligible for a refill but I needed the drugs. I grabbed a gun and went to a nearby pharmacy. I sat outside that store for about an hour. Finally, I decided that the best thing I could do would be to break away from the addictive drugs. I went home, went through some withdrawal sickness, and started planning my strategy.

It took me another two years to successfully get free. However, without cannabis, I don't think I would have been able to conquer the addiction.

Due to the cost, and inconsistencies of buying marijuana

on the black market, I learned how to grow it. I was already unknowingly using it as a medicine to relieve my monthly withdrawal symptoms. Growing cannabis was the only way I could afford to use it, and this also became part of my therapy.

Then, I began learning that medical marijuana could help with eliminating opioid addiction while reducing withdrawal symptoms and providing natural pain relief. I discovered that there was proven science backing up marijuana as medicine. I researched cannabis and hemp: their uses, benefits, and side effects, and how cannabinoids help the human body create homeostasis naturally, without side effects, addiction, or overdose issues.

Twelve years after beginning my journey with opioids, I was able to beat the addiction using medical marijuana and changing to a mostly natural-food diet. Medical marijuana helped reduce my drug withdrawal symptoms, enabling me to eliminate opioids, and I credit it with saving my life. I have been pharmaceutical free since 2016.

Because of my success using medical marijuana, I decided that I wanted to help educate others about how it might be able to help them with their own health issues.

I've been an advocate for medical marijuana legalization since 2014. I have lobbied senators, traveled state-wide to speak on behalf of the cannabis community, and appeared in local forums to share my journey and bring people's awareness to the benefits of medical marijuana.

I am continually asked "How does marijuana work?" and "What is the difference between marijuana and medical marijuana?" They are one and the same; it's all cannabis.

Many people, including those in the media, are confused by the hype that CBD is getting. There is very scientific information available, as well as how-to-get-high information and marijuana-is-bad-for-you information. But it is difficult to find simple, easy-to-understand rules for medicating with cannabis.

This is where I can help. With this booklet, my goal is to dispel some myths while educating you on a plant that has numerous health benefits. Cannabis has improved my life, and in the following pages, I hope you'll see how it could improve yours.

1

Introduction

It really puzzles me to see marijuana connected with narcotics…dope and all that crap. It's a thousand times better than whiskey—it's an assistant—a friend. —Louis Armstrong

Congratulations! You did it! You've taken the first step toward gaining knowledge that could save your life, or the life of a loved one.

You now have a booklet that explains some of the mystery and confusion around an amazing plant and an all-natural medicine. Cannabis—medical marijuana—is saving lives every day. Every day, someone stops taking deadly, addicting, synthetic pain medicine. They are able to overcome the highly addictive drug's deadly grasp by medicating naturally with cannabis.

There is so much information about this amazing plant, and scientific research has not even scratched the surface. I'm hopeful that with just the basic facts I provide, you will realize cannabis is a life-giving plant, not the demon weed we've been warned about.

This booklet provides a foundation for your journey into cannabis. You will learn a little about the 20,000-year history of hemp use. I will explain my views on why marijuana and hemp became illegal. If you like government and elitist conspiracy theories, check out Chapter 3. Then, in Chapter 5, I cover the basics of how cannabis works with the human body using the endocannabinoid system. Finally, I go over how to purchase and medicate with cannabis.

My wish for you is that after reading this booklet, you will realize that humans have been consuming hemp since the beginning of time. Taking it out of our diets through prohibition has removed vital nutrients from our bodies and had negative consequences on our health. The prevalence of cancer, diabetes, poor blood circulation, and chronic inflammation has increased. All these increases in disease began shortly after cannabis prohibition. Could there be a connection? In my opinion, definitely!

2

It's Called Cannabis

I think people need to be educated to the fact that marijuana is not a drug.
Marijuana is an herb. God put it here. —Willie Nelson

Cannabis and hemp are both in the *cannabis sativa* plant family. They are similar, with one distinct difference: cannabis contains the cannabinoid THC (tetrahydrocannabinol). While hemp has only trace amounts of THC, it has a much higher percentage of the cannabinoid CBD (cannabidiol). Because cannabis contains THC, it is considered the more medicinal variety of the plant. THC helps create the pain relief benefits that marijuana provides. However, to improve marijuana's healing abilities and medicinal benefits, it is now being bred with higher levels of CBD as well.

It's important to understand that *using the whole plant is what can heal you*. Try to not focus on just THC and CBD. Using the whole plant is the only way to receive all the benefits marijuana provides.

Hemp is the more industrial variety of cannabis. According to Google, it has more than 20,000 uses. It has many valuable applications, including enhancing livestock feed, fabric, oil, fuel, health supplements, rope, even plastics and concrete. Hemp is also a phytoremediation plant: it can remove toxins from the soil while returning good nutrients back to it. It is one of the most beneficial plants in nature and should not be criminalized.

3

The History of Cannabis

Some of my finest hours have been spent on my back veranda, smoking
hemp and observing as far as my eye can see. —Thomas Jefferson

All varieties of cannabis have been used medicinally for centuries. The earliest known use of medical marijuana dates to 2500 BC, in Asia. Marijuana was discovered in the medicine pouch of a shaman. Hemp has been found in almost every ancient civilization, and it may even be listed in the Bible as Kaneh-Bosem (Exodus 30: 22-23), one of the ingredients in holy anointing oil.

Throughout history, cannabis and hemp have provided nutrients and medicine for humanity. Because hemp had so many uses, in America in the 1700s, farmers were required to dedicate at least one acre of farmland to growing it. In England, King Henry VIII required one acre per 60 acres of farmland devoted to hemp. After prohibition began, in 1937, the cultivation of hemp was again temporarily permitted, during World War II (1942-1944). Hemp was processed to make rope, assisting the war effort.

Sadly, the ability to grow hemp or produce cannabis has also been used as a political tool to control the masses. The *only* times in history when cannabis was prohibited were periods in which one group of people was trying to control another.

4

The Great Cannabis Conspiracy

Herb is the healing of a nation, alcohol is the destruction. —
Bob Marley

I will give you one example of how the prohibition of cannabis was used to control a segment of the population. Feel free to search for more examples, as they are out there, dating back to the 1300s.

In America during the 1930s, Mexican immigrants and African Americans, specifically, black jazz musicians, were considered a threat to white society. They were also associated with smoking marijuana, which is similar to hemp.

The conspiracy theory is that hemp was just about to create serious competition in the oil, fabric, paper, and lumber industries, as well as other commercial markets, due to a recently discovered, less-expensive processing method.

The Randolph Hearst family controlled the timber and paper industries. Hearst also owned newspapers that ran anti-cannabis propaganda campaigns. The media has always been full of fake news. Just as it is today, the media, mostly newspapers, had influence over public opinion, and they ran many stories on the horrors of marijuana.

Lamont DuPont, CEO of the DuPont company, and Andrew Mellon (the nation's wealthiest man), who were running the chemical industries, were concerned that this new processing method would severely cut into their monopolies. These large family conglomerates got together and decided to raise the public's fear of marijuana, including hemp, and also breed fear of immigrants and minorities. You know, kill two birds with one stone: control the Hispanic and black populations while making hemp illegal through its association with marijuana, eliminating the threat to the families' established businesses. This is just one example of a wealthy conglomerate with an ingenious business plan for putting survival, and profits, over American lives. Other industries have implemented similar strategies.

The businesses or families used their power and influence to control the media, and they went as far as to have a family relative, Harry Anslinger, nominated as America's first drug czar. Soon after this, in 1937, cannabis was deemed illegal, and the rest, as they say, is history.

I have shared this theory with you because I believe it to be mostly true. American politicians and corporate interests have lied to us and the world. Most of the world has prohibited cannabis use based on pressure from the United States. Countries that belong to the United Nations have all signed the Single Convention on Narcotic Drugs treaty (1961), which prohibits rights to marijuana use based on the assumption, not scientific research, that it is harmful.

The United States federal government has studied the "negative" effects of cannabis since the 1970s. Government research conducted at the University of Mississippi revealed very few negative effects. However, scientific studies have not been focused on discovering the benefits of cannabis use. Research has been designed to prove that marijuana is harmful. If cannabis were bad for your health, wouldn't a 50-year federal government study prove it? Imagine if we could have studied the health *benefits* of cannabis for all those years instead.

With new laws being passed every year, cannabis legislation is changing along with mainstream attitudes. I believe that one day, cannabis and hemp will be used to benefit humanity legally, not to control people or just get them high.

Now that you know how hemp became illegal, it's time to learn how it can heal you.

You're probably wondering how cannabis works with your body. It is amazing, and valid scientific research has only just begun. This is an extremely exciting time for hemp and cannabis research.

5
Health Benefits

Smoking marijuana . . . is certainly no more damaging than having a drink,
and I suspect it's better for you than having a drink. —
Richard Branson

Throughout history, hemp has been required to be grown for its value. Ship sails, as well as clothing, were made from the fabric. People could burn the oil, use it as medicine, and eat it. It was also used as livestock feed. All the amazing nutrients and cannabinoids (we'll get to these in a minute) were fed to livestock, which people then ate. Which, in my opinion, means that people were eating CBD and more than 100 other cannabinoids every time they ate meat. Today cows, chickens, pigs, fish, and turkeys are mostly fed GMO corn and soy products loaded with chemical fertilizers, pesticides, herbicides, antibiotics, and hormones. Yuck!

Here is a comparison of corn and hemp seed nutritional values:

	Corn nutrients	Hemp seed nutrients
Calories	177	111
Fiber	4.6g	2g
Protein	5.4g	6.3g
Fat	7.9g	9. g
Carbs	41g	2.6g
Sodium	8.2mg	0
Potassium	205mg	240mg
Magnesium	211mg	140mg
Phosphorous	349mg	330mg
Zinc	1.1mg	1.9mg

Iron	4.5mg	1.6mg
Vitamins	A, B-6, C, K	A, B-1, -3, -6; C, D, E, K

*Statistics taken from various online sources. Values are for hemp seeds. Cannabis would have more nutrients; currently the statistics are not verifiable. However, plants are known to be more nutritious than seeds.

Cannabis contains the perfect balance of Omega 3, 6, and 9. A 3-1-1 ratio is optimal for people. Corn contains higher amounts of the omegas, which could be unhealthy. Cannabis also has a variety of terpenes, micronutrients, phytonutrients, and more than 100 cannabinoids that interact with our bodies.

Imagine how healthy cattle would be if they were fed hemp instead of corn. We could possibly even eliminate hormones and antibiotics from their diet. Cattle would not be the only ones to benefit; so, would we. When you add the health value of cannabinoids, the benefits far outweigh those of using corn for livestock feed.

In warm climates you can get multiple crops per year, unlike with corn, which allows for only one crop a year.

The fact is that cannabis and hemp are incredibly nutritional, and they can heal our bodies, as well as the soil.

They make excellent livestock feed and are inexpensive to produce. In addition, hemp has more than 20,000 other uses. Cannabis is a natural medicine that increases homeostasis in the human body. To me, it just makes sense to have them in our lives.

Here is a list of claims about the health benefits of cannabis. Some have not been proven by scientific research. However, I have met hundreds of people who make these claims, and they are convinced that cannabis is what healed or helps them. Google "cannabis health benefits" and you will find thousands of claims.

Reduces muscle spasms	Multiple sclerosis relief	Relieves nausea
Chemotherapy drug relief	Increases appetite	Relieves seizures
Relieves symptoms of Crohn's disease	Relieves chronic pain	Drug withdrawal relief
Calms attention deficit hyperactivity disorder (ADHD)/attentio n deficit disorder (ADD)	Calms Post-traumatic stress disorder (PTSD)	ALS relief
Antidepressant	Anti-cancer benefits	Assists in controlling Epilepsy seizures

Regulates diabetes	Calms autism	Maintains homeostasis
Relieves glaucoma issues	Arthritis pain relief	Fibromyalgia pain relief
Slows Alzheimer's disease	Insomnia relief	May reduce skin cancers
Assists in treating anorexia	Improves lupus symptoms	Relieves Dravet syndrome symptoms
Alleviates anxiety	May improve lung health	Quickens healing process

6

Cannabinoids and the Endocannabinoid System

Marijuana is beneficial to many patients. —Dr. Jocelyn Elders

What is a cannabinoid, and where can you find one? Do you need them? What is the endocannabinoid system (ECS)? Even after 10 years of self-education, I don't fully understand what a cannabinoid is, and neither do scientists. It has been illegal to research cannabis for the past 80 years, so there is a lot of catching up to do. The science is complex, there is much to know, and this booklet can only give you some basics that, I hope, demonstrate why cannabis and hemp should be included in your war chest for health and happiness. Hold on to your seat because you might get blown away.

The ECS is a complex system that follows a path in your body similar to that of your central nervous system. That's right, folks. The endocannabinoid system touches every part of your body. It seems odd that a system within us, which has a connection to everything in our bodies, was only discovered in 1992. It was discovered when scientists in Israel were trying to understand why cannabis has so many positive attributes while having very few, if any, negative side effects. You might want to read that again: Scientists Dr. Lumir Hanus and Dr. William Devane of Israel were trying to understand why cannabis has so many positive attributes while having very few, if any, negative side effects.

If you interpret that as I do, you realize they are saying cannabis is a nearly perfect plant that, when consumed in its natural state, has few, if any, negative side effects.

Humans are not unique in having an ECS. As a matter of fact, all living things with vertebrae have one. This system is responsible for regulating nearly every vital bodily function. The ECS ensures that your body can maintain homeostasis. Without it, you would never be balanced.

The science is still very new, and there is a lot to learn. We know that there are at least two cannabinoid receptors, CB1 and CB2, which react to molecules called cannabinoids. CB1 receptors are found mainly in the brain, and they follow the central nervous system. They are also in the lungs, liver, and kidneys. CB2 receptors are found in the blood and bones. Think of the CB1 and CB2 receptors as being like nerve endings: they are everywhere in your body, interacting with every part of you. They receive cannabinoids and put them to work regulating your body. These molecules help regulate everything your body needs to function in complete homeostasis. Cannabinoids ensure that your body is balanced. There are more than 100 known cannabinoids in the cannabis plant, including THC and CBD.

About now, you may be asking yourself, "What is a cannabinoid?" That is a great question. It is "a chemical compound that acts on our CB receptors (the ECS). Cannabinoids activate your ECS to maintain internal stability and health. They mediate communication between cells, and when there is a deficiency or problem with the ECS, unpleasant symptoms and physical complications occur."

Cannabinoids create homeostasis, or balance, in your body. Your ECS is unique in that it is designed to react specifically to the cannabinoids in marijuana. These natural chemicals provide balance to all other systems in your body. This fact tells us that cannabis contributes to overall health. Without cannabinoids and your ECS, you would never be in complete balance. Never. The ECS is designed so that the body can work at a more perfect level. You can reach pure homeostasis, but it's much easier with cannabis in your body.

7
Objections Answered

[Marijuana] doesn't have a high potential for abuse, and there are very legitimate medical applications. In fact, sometimes marijuana is the only thing that works.
—Dr. Sanjay Gupta

You may be thinking:
1. I've been told my whole life that marijuana makes me dumb and lazy.
2. Politicians and uneducated doctors tell us that we don't smoke medicine.
3. I do not want to feel high.

To address the first statement, it has been scientifically proven that cannabis does not kill brain cells. It actually supports brain cell activity. In studies, cannabis has been shown to have some success in reducing and preventing Alzheimer's disease. It does *not* make you dumb and lazy. The dumb and lazy stereotypes come from the media and misconstrued social norms. I know many cannabis consumers who are athletes, lawyers, doctors, business owners, and other successful people. They are the exact opposite of dumb and lazy. Many professional athletes, including Michael Phelps, 23-time Olympic gold medal winner, admit to consuming cannabis. I believe that winning 23 gold medals over several years kind of validates the usefulness of cannabis as a health supplement.

To combat the objection that "We don't smoke medicine," here is something most folks don't realize: cannabis, when smoked, provides medicinal benefits. It helps relax the mind and body better than Xanax or Valium, without the deadly addiction hazards (every year, 11,000 people in America die taking anti-anxiety drugs). It can reduce hyperactivity, ADD, and ADHD. It reduces phlegm in ALS patients, and has been studied to determine its ability to increase airway and lung capacity. It has been proven to *not* be linked to lung cancer. Cannabis has been known to increase appetite and relieve nausea, and it is used with cancer patients to relieve negative side effects of chemotherapy. I know from my own life experience that cannabis can reduce or eliminate the need for synthetic pain pills. It is also an amazing withdrawal-symptom reliever, and it may alleviate many asthma symptoms.

If you Google "health benefits of cannabis," you will find thousands of crazy stories. Many of them are nonsense, but a lot of them are true. The best way to learn about cannabis is to read about the plant and what it can do to help you. Snopes.com is a good place to check online facts. Then, try it.

CBD limits the amount of THC allowed to react with your body. This cellular communication ensures that you cannot overdose when using cannabis naturally. Cannabis has never killed anyone, ever. It is one of the safest plants you can put in your body. You can experiment and find out what works best for you.

A really cool thing that many people don't know about cannabis, and hemp to a smaller degree, is that consumed in their raw form, they are superfoods. Their nutrient benefits rival kale and blueberries.

Now on to statement number 3, "I do not want to feel high." Uncooked and unprocessed marijuana will provide you with vitamins, minerals, micronutrients, terpenes, cannabinoids, Phyto cannabinoids, phytonutrients, and more. Cannabis, when consumed raw, will not make you high. Cannabis consumed raw might actually be better for you than eating kale, and I think you know that kale has an awesome amount of nutrients.

In order for marijuana to get you high, it must be heated to over 215 degrees. When the plant material is heated, a chemical reaction occurs, turning THCA and CBDA into THC and CBD. Only when marijuana is heated does the plant create the high feeling associated with smoking it.

Eating raw cannabis daily can improve your health drastically, because the nutrients in cannabis are designed to help your body remain in perfect homeostasis (balance).

You are probably wondering: Because marijuana has been illegal, where has your body gotten the chemicals (cannabinoids) to activate the balancing effects on your ECS? The simple answer is that other plants can simulate or mimic cannabinoids. A Phyto cannabinoid is "any plant-derived natural product capable of either directly interacting with cannabinoid receptors or sharing a chemical similarity with cannabinoids or both" (National Center for Biotechnology Information). A cannabimimetic is "any substance with similar or mimicking pharmacological effects to those of Cannabis." These are recently discovered compounds that can react with both CB1 and CB2 receptors.

Several plants can interact with your body's ECS. However, cannabis seems to be specifically designed to connect to your ECS and CB receptors. Your body is designed to process cannabinoids specifically from the cannabis plant. I hope you can see that cannabis and your ECS are a perfect match. Notice that the definition of cannabimimetic states that other plants have *similar*, or *mimicking* effects on your ECS. Cannabis is specifically targeting your ECS. Other plants try to adapt to it. Which one do you think will work the best: a plant specifically designed for a system that touches every area of your body, or a plant that must adapt to work with your body? Cannabis is the only plant I know of that is specifically designed for operating with your ECS.

Other foods can stimulate your CB receptors:

- **Black pepper:** We are finding out through science that black pepper assists the body in absorbing nutrients, and also reacts with the ECS.
- **Clove:** It can mimic cannabis and react with your CB receptors.
- **Sunflower** (*Helichrysum* variety) and sunflower lecithin aid your body's ability to absorb nutrients more efficiently and may react with CB receptors.

- **Echinacea** has a cannabinoid that reacts with the CB2 receptors and helps strengthen the immune system, as well as reduce inflammation and pain. Side note: echinacea makes a great tea for colds and coughs.
- **Flax seed** contains CBD and some other cannabinoids. The amounts are not as concentrated as in cannabis, but they are present. So, until marijuana is legal in your state, you can eat a whole gob lot of flaxseed to meet your CBD needs.
- **Chocolate** (preferably dark) reacts with your ECS. It helps you relax. (Unfortunately, the refined sugar in chocolate makes you *not* relax.)
- **Hops:** Yes, the stuff you make beer with has some minor cannabinoids in it. No wonder beer makes people happy.

- **Black truffles** contain anandamide, a chemical that reacts with your ECS and can activate your CB receptors in similar ways as cannabis. Anandamide makes you feel happy.

As you can see, there are ways to naturally activate your ECS without cannabis. However, cannabis is the only plant I know of that is specifically helpful with maintaining the ECS. I believe that to reach perfect balance in our bodies, we should incorporate cannabis or hemp in our diets.

How do you know what to buy? What is the best way to use cannabis for perfect health? In the next chapter, I will try to dispel some myths and give you the facts about purchasing CBD and medical marijuana.

8

The CBD Scam

"CBD helps with pain, stress, and anxiety. It has the benefits of marijuana without the high".
—Jennifer Aniston, Us magazine

First off, I know that CBD alone is helping many people heal from many different ailments. I also know that the placebo effect is real, and maybe some of the healing is related to positive thoughts. There is a lot of media coverage about CBD, which is quickly becoming a major superfood, super supplement, and super drug.

You need to be aware of a couple of issues. My first concern is that the media is only promoting an exceedingly small piece of the cannabis story. CBD is a newly discovered—yet, not completely understood—compound in the cannabis plant. It is only one of hundreds of nutrients in cannabis and hemp. I cannot stress this enough: CBD is only one of more than 100 cannabinoids, as well as vitamins, minerals, micronutrients, phytonutrients, and fiber.

Cannabis has amazing benefits as a "whole plant." If you are just taking CBD, you're missing out on most of the plant's benefits. When companies extract only the CBD, you don't get all the other nutrients that cannabis provides. When you're sick and drink orange juice to feel better, is it only the vitamin C that heals you? Or is it all the natural nutrients found in an orange, working with your body, that keep you healthy?

When buying CBD products, keep in mind that hemp seed oil contains about 1/100th of the benefits that the whole plant oil contains. Seeds are just not a great source of nutrients. Hemp seed oil is about as beneficial as olive oil and coconut oil. Yes, it's nutritious, but not worth all the attention it's gotten. It is certainly not worth $40 an ounce unless the container is made of crystal.

When purchasing CBD in an oil or lotion, look for the term's *entourage effect*, *full spectrum*, and *whole plant*. These phrases indicate when the entire plant was used in the processing of the product. If the label says only hemp seed, walk away.

Nutritionally speaking, hemp is lower in benefits compared with cannabis. As noted earlier, it makes for an amazing livestock feed, oil, and fabric, and it has 20,000 other uses. Cannabis is the most medicinal of the genus, just as holy basil (Tulsi) is more medicinal than other varieties of basil. If you're looking for pain relief, or, should I say, more immediate pain relief, you really do need the THC as well. CBD is just one piece of the solution that cannabis provides. But the whole plant will keep you balanced. It will allow your body to reach homeostasis. Let me say this: You cannot reach perfect balance without activating the CB1 and CB2 receptors in your ECS. Cannabis is the only plant I know of that specifically works with your ECS. I believe this tells us that cannabis and hemp should be part of our daily diets.

Another thing to consider is the carrier oil: the type of oil infused with the CBD. It could be coconut, olive, grapeseed, or medium chain triglycerides (MCT). MCT oil is really just oil with high fat content. Cannabis nutrients like to attach to the fat cells in oil. Higher fat content means better extraction. The carrier oil has a lot to do with the health benefits. I personally feel that raw, organic, unfiltered coconut oil is the best for extracting cannabis; it is a "super oil."

Many people I know get overly concerned about the total milligrams of CBD per package or per serving.

I want this to be perfectly clear and simple for you. There are about a dozen ways that the milligrams are calculated, and there are no set standards. So, every company is calculating this number a little differently. And no one is verifying what companies are claiming.

Secondly, companies test only about 10 percent of the entire crop used to make the oil. Every seed produces a slightly different plant (just as every human is slightly different). When they figure out the dosage, the numbers may not be accurate. And again, there are no standards for how the milligrams are calculated, so you never really know how accurate those numbers are.

Until we get some oversight, just forget about milligrams of CBD. If you must know, an average adult would probably need between 15 and 25 milligrams a day. However, no one knows that as a fact. So, forget about milligrams. Focus on the type of oil and how the product was made.

CBD alone will not make you high. Most likely, you won't immediately feel any different. You may be receiving some benefits from the placebo effect. When medicating naturally, your body needs time to absorb the nutrients. CBD will improve how your body works, but first it has to get into your body. It takes a little time for your body to absorb and begin using the nutrients effectively. It will take a little time for you to notice how good you feel.

I strongly believe that cannabis should be in our bodies. However, today it is a new fad, so the price is ridiculous. Forty dollars or more for an ounce of plant oil is crazy. What you need to know is that cannabis and hemp crops can be harvested twice a year in warm climates. That's a "whole gob lot" of plant material. You only get one crop of olives, and how much does olive oil cost? A lot less. Both are plant based, both are great for you. Hemp is much less expensive to grow and harvest than olives.

Saffron, also a plant, is the world's most expensive spice. Saffron has a lot of health benefits, including as an anti-inflammatory, antidepressant, antioxidant, and cancer fighter. It is incredibly difficult to grow and harvest. It must be harvested by hand, while hemp is machine processed. It takes about 5,000 flowers to produce one ounce of the spice. It also takes about 12 hours to pick 5,000 flowers. The price of saffron is about $40 an ounce. It takes 10 times more work to grow saffron than it does to grow and process hemp. The two plants have similar benefits (minus cannabinoids), so why are they the same price per ounce? Mind boggling!

Raw cannabis will not make you feel high. Raw cannabis is extremely nutrient rich, and, taken daily, will improve your health, but so will coconut oil and olive oil. Coconut oil costs about 50 cents per ounce. Cannabis-infused coconut oil shouldn't cost more than a dollar an ounce. But because heating the oil could make you high, it costs around $40 or more an ounce.

I'm hopeful that once America opens its eyes and legalizes the plant for everyone, the price will reflect the amount of work it takes to produce. My question is why it costs so much more than comparable crops. That should be your question, as well.

If you're thinking about medicating with cannabis or hemp, I recommend one or two full eye droppers (about 2 ml) of cannabis oil (where legal) twice a day to start. If it's not legal, I recommend whole plant, full spectrum, or entourage CBD made with coconut oil, or pure hemp oil from the plant (not from seeds). The entourage effect is when all parts of the plant are used in processing a product naturally. You are looking for products that use all parts of the plant.

After two weeks, evaluate how you feel. Has anything changed? If not, add a third dose and wait another week. After about a month, you should be able to cut down to one dose a day, or a maintenance dose every couple of days.

Within 30 days, you should be feeling more energetic, more balanced, and happier. Your body should begin to function better. Your digestion, blood circulation, and concentration should all improve. You really will just feel better because your body is reaching homeostasis. This is a very cool place for your body to be.

A Trip to the Dispensary

If you substitute marijuana for tobacco and alcohol, you'll add eight to 24 years to your life. —Jack Herer

So, you've decided to start medicating naturally with cannabis. But how, exactly, do you do that? Perhaps you've never tried cannabis or purchased it legally and walking into a dispensary can be very intimidating. What is an edible, a tincture, a vape cartridge? How does each work, and how much does it cost?

I will try to answer some of these questions.

There are many ways to consume medical marijuana. New consumption methods are always being developed and introduced to the market.

The most basic consumption method is smoking raw cannabis flowers, or buds. This raw plant material is dried and cured to perfection for your enjoyment. You can smoke it, you can eat it, you can cook with it. Smoking dried flowers is what most people associate with using cannabis, and it is my preferred method of medicating. An average marijuana cigarette (a "joint") contains about half a gram of dried flowers. It will cost you $5-20 per gram.

However, not all states allow raw cannabis to be sold. In that case, you can buy oils, edibles, herbal tinctures, or pills.

Tinctures

Herbal tinctures are probably the most common consumption method for new cannabis consumers looking for an easy, discreet way to medicate.

The use of tinctures dates back thousands of years. Folk medicine is full of recipes for tinctures made from plants.

These easy-to-use liquids cost $40-160 an ounce, based mostly on the milligrams of THC or CBD in them.

Tinctures are made with various oils or with alcohol. The plant material is soaked in liquid for up to 30 days, which brings out the good nutrients—you know, the cannabinoids, vitamins, minerals, and more.

I would normally say that oil tinctures would be the most nutritionally beneficial for the average person. However, alcohol extracts more nutrients from the plant. A squirt or two of the alcohol tincture under your tongue, and within 20 minutes, you should notice a change in your body. They can give you a feeling of euphoria. You may feel a little dizzy. After all, you are placing close to 100% alcohol in your body, as well as THC. I will caution you that alcohol tinctures cause a burning sensation in your mouth like that of drinking hard liquor straight. An oil tincture won't burn your mouth. Remember, it is the whole plant that heals you, not just the THC and CBD.

Vape cartridges

Vaping cartridges filled with plant oil are usually a fairly strong means of medicating. You can also vape only hemp, which contains only CBD, to eliminate the high feeling you get from THC. The oil in the cartridge is very thick. It is usually pure plant oil; some dispensaries refer to this as a concentrate, or distillate. Cartridges list varying milligrams. The lower the milligrams of THC, the less high you will feel. If you are looking for pain relief, pay attention to the percentage of THC. I have seen THC amounts as high as 90 percent on vape cartridges. THC at these percentages is crazy strong medicine and should really only be used for severe pain.

If you are just looking for health benefits from CBD, the human body needs only an estimated 15-25 mg of CBD a day.

Edibles

You can also medicate by consuming edibles: candies, cookies, other foods, and drinks infused with the plant oil. Although it is a little harder to determine the correct dose when eating cannabis, edibles are an excellent way to receive the health benefits from the plant.

With edibles, it takes longer for you to feel the effects. It could take up to 1-1/2 hours to get relief. It just depends on how fast your body can process the ingredients.

Pills and suppositories

Suppositories are alternatives to smoking. With suppositories, as with smoking, the cannabis directly enters your bloodstream and then moves on to your brain, whereas edibles, including pills, must be digested, and processed by your body before entering your bloodstream.

Topicals

Lotions, sprays, and oils can all be infused with cannabis and hemp. Topicals are great; they may reduce swelling, aches, and pains, as well as heal cuts sooner. I highly recommend them.

Putting cannabis on your skin will not make you high. Applying cannabis to your skin can be beneficial for skin health. However, to immediately relieve pain, you need to include the whole plant, which contains THC. CBD alone is not always a quick pain reliever, and it needs time to work with your body.

To keep it simple at the dispensary, remember that the whole plant is what will heal you. Always ask "Is this product made from the whole plant?" If they say "Yes, but we add the terpenes back in after extraction," you are not getting the whole plant medicine; you're getting something made in a laboratory.

In my opinion, we should all be consuming raw cannabis flowers every day in our food or as tinctures. I smoke it daily for its relaxing anti-anxiety effects, as well as the health benefits. Over time you learn to control the giggles and munchies. LOL.

10

Continuing Education

Smoking weed doesn't make you paranoid. Weed being illegal makes you paranoid.
—Snoop Dogg

I hope our short journey into the mysterious world of cannabis has opened your eyes to the health benefits of this amazing plant. In my opinion, the benefits far outweigh any negative side effects, which may include slight anxiety, paranoia, and feeling tired. At high doses, you may feel some disorientation. However, most unpleasant negative side effects can often be eliminated by having a cup of coffee, taking a shower, or just relaxing for a few minutes. Take some deep breaths and try to relax.

Cannabis and hemp are amazing plants that can heal you and help balance your body. Cannabinoids help your body create homeostasis naturally, without creating damaging side effects, addiction, or overdose issues.

Think about the information I've provided in this booklet and continue educating yourself on the benefits of cannabis, an herb that heals and brings homeostasis to your body. Embracing cannabis as a health supplement can assist your body and mind in becoming balanced, and, when you use it responsibly, make your life happier.

Know these simple truths and get healthier and happier medicating with all-natural cannabis.

11

Resources

The resources listed here are a small segment of the available knowledge on cannabis. I have spent 10 years researching cannabis and hemp, using Google as a starting point and then diving deeper to find as much truth as possible. Use these resources to get further educated on your journey to cannabis health.

- advancedholistichealth.com (history of hemp)
- cdc.gov (Centers for Disease Control)
- charlottesweb.com (the "original" CBD plant; great information)
- dea.gov (Drug Enforcement Administration)

- drugabuse.com (mainstream drug information)
- drughistory.org (statement by Harry Anslinger)
- echoconnection.org (excellent source for cannabis education)
- encyclopedia.com (super site for mainstream information)
- forbes.com (some good articles on cannabis, hemp, CBD, and more)
- google.com
- healer.com (Dr. Dustin Sulak, excellent medical marijuana education)
- health.harvard.edu (various studies)
- healthline.com (great source for all health information)
- hemplifestylenetwork.com (All things hemp)
- hightimes.com (The original marijuana magazine, still going strong)
- leafly.com (in-depth general cannabis information)
- livescience.com (multiple articles)
- mayoclinic.org (So many studies with both positive and negative conclusions about cannabis)
- medicalnewstoday.com (health stories)

- narconon.org (history of cannabis use)
- ncbi.nlm.nih.gov (National Center for Biotechnology Information; tons of research)
- newsone.com (story on Michael Phelps)
- norml.org (National Organization for the Reform of Marijuana Laws. Has been a leader in the cannabis community since the 1970s)
- pbs.org (multiple stories)
- projectcbd.com (all things hemp/CBD)
- sciencedirect.com (almost 1 million articles on health)
- thcliving.co (All things marijuana)
- *The Emperor Wears No Clothes* by Jack Herer
- webmd.com (one of my sources for verifying alternative health claims)
- wikipedia.org
- who.int (World Health Organization)

Speaking Engagements

Stephen is available to share his journey and insights with your organization. For more information, contact him at StephenRadentz@yahoo.com, balancedbynature.net, or (561) 889-8346

www.ingramcontent.com/pod-product-compliance
Lightning Source LLC
Chambersburg PA
CBHW021117020426
42331CB00004B/529